One Among Many Members

A Biblical Evaluation of Individualism

By Ian Kissell

A Master of Theology thesis submitted to Dallas Theological Seminary

May, 2016

Readers: Scott Horrell & Lanier Burns

TABLE OF CONTENTS

CHAPTER 1

INTRODUCTION

Individualism: An Introduction

Jesus loves me! this I know, For the Bible tells me so;
Little ones to Him belong, They are weak, but He is strong.
Yes, Jesus loves me, Yes, Jesus loves me,
Yes, Jesus loves me, The Bible tells me so.

This short hymn, written by Anna Bartlett Warner, and first published in 1860, is a familiar favorite in English speaking Christian homes and churches—but is it correct? Specifically, does God love *me*, as the song claims, or does He simply love us? If God loves His church, does that necessarily mean that He loves me specifically?

Though seemingly innocuous, this ditty reaches directly to the heart of the question of the relationship of Christianity to individualism, a cultural outlook which some commentators have claimed is the defining mark of Western civilization.[1] Harry Triandis, a leading expert in the area, notes that the individualism-collectivism dichotomy might be "the most significant cultural difference among cultures."[2] Individualism first appears as a technical term in the political and ideological musing of the 19th century.

[1] Richard Koch, "Is Individualism Good or Bad?," Huffpost Business Blog, entry posted October 7, 2013, http://www.huffingtonpost.com/richard-koch/is-individualism-good-or-_b_4056305.html (accessed January 26, 2016). Richard Koch holds an M.A. from Oxford University and is a bestselling author in the disciplines of business, management, and entrepreneurship.

[2] Harry C. Triandis, "Individualism-Collectivism and Personality," *Journal of Personality* 69 (2001): 907.

Advanced by French, German, and English philosophers and political thinkers alike, although each with a different bent, it can clearly be seen in the 1789 French *Declaration of the Rights of Man.* This document, which served as a pillar of French Revolution ideology, begins with the first declaration that "Men are born and remain free and equal in rights," and continues to assert that "Liberty consists in the ability to do whatever does not harm another; hence the exercise of the natural rights of each man has no other limits than those which assure to other members of society the enjoyment of the same rights."[3] Arguing from "natural right," this radical declaration of the freedom of the individual articulated the changing climate of Western culture.

The term *individualism* was "First coined by conservatives like Robert Palmer in England and Louis de Bonald and Joseph de Maistre in France to designate the disintegration of society which they believed had resulted from the French Revolution and its doctrine of individual rights."[4] Individualism has since become a scapegoat for all of Western society's ills. Typically framed as a Western versus Eastern cultural dispute,[5] if there is

---

[3] *Declaration of the Rights of Man*, articles 1 and 4.

[4] Albert W. Musschenga, in *The Many Faces of Individualism,* eds. Anton von Harskamp and Albert W. Musschenga (Leuven: Peeters, 2001), 4; Cigdem Kagıtçıbası, "Individualism and Collectivism," in *Social Behaviors and Application,* vol. 3 of *Handbook of Cross-Cultural Psychology,* ed. John Berry et al., 2nd ed., (Boston: Allyn and Bacon, 1997), 3–4.

[5] "It is typical to examine individualism and collectivism through comparisons between the cultures of the West, presumed to reflect individualism, and those of the East, presumed to reflect collectivism." E. E. Sampson, "Reinterpreting Individualism and Collectivism: Their Religious Roots and Monologic versus Dialogic Person-Other Relationship," *American Psychologist* 55 (2000): 1425; Triandis, "Individualism-Collectivism and Personality," 908; E. Zerubavel and E. R. Smith, "Transcending Cognitive Individualism," *Social Psychology Quarterly* 73 (2010): 321.

some aspect of Western society which a social critic deems lacking, individualism is most likely to blame. Nineteenth century French political thinker Alexis de Tocqueville comments in His classic work *Democracy in America* that

> Individualism proceeds from erroneous judgment more than from depraved feelings; it originates as much in the deficiencies of the mind as in the perversity of the heart. . . . Individualism, at first, only saps the virtue of public life; but, in the long run, it attacks and destroys all others, and is at length absorbed in downright egotism.[6]

Individualism has not escaped criticism among Christian thinkers as well. A whole host of theologians have attributed much of Western Christianity's ills to the prevalence of individualism in the mindsets of Western Christianity.[7]

Defining Individualism

Individualism is notoriously difficult to define, largely because it can be a technical term which transcends disciplines, and thus lacks a consistent definition. As David Miller bemoans, "The word itself is employed extensively by politicians, economists, educators, theologians, sociologists . . . and many others. Yet no one, as far as I can find, has taken the time to formulate a clear and accurate conception of what individualism means

---

[6] Alexis de Tocqueville, *Democracy in America*, trans. Henry Reeve, vol. 2 (New York: J. & H. G. Langley, 1840), 585.

[7] For an example, Cf. John Kavanaugh, "Autonomous Individualism," *America* 196 (2007): 8.

when used in its proper sense."[8] Although writing in 1967, Miller's words are almost prophetic—now in the 21st century, the picture is hardly much clearer. Ethicist Albert Musschenga agrees on the point, stating that "Individualism refers to certain changes in society and their undesirable consequences but also to behavioral patterns, attitudes, and values. Therefore, it has to be replaced by a more refined vocabulary."[9]

Boulding's Hierarchy of Systems

Kenneth Boulding identifies a nine-tiered hierarchy of systems: (1) static frameworks, (2) dynamic systems with predetermined motions, (3) cybernetic systems which react to information, (4) self-controlling systems, (5) living plants, (6) animals, (7) individual human beings, (8) human organizations and society, and (9) transcendental systems.[10] Individualism and collectivism are theories which concern the relationship between levels seven and eight. Corporate human systems—be they families, businesses or religious organizations, or cultures—all involve the incorporation of human beings into larger social frameworks. Neither individualism nor collectivism seeks to deny the existence of levels seven or eight in Boulding's hierarchy. Rather, they differently emphasize the relative value of one these two tiers. The significant of this point cannot be overstated for this discussion. It is not sufficient to merely affirm that both individuals and collectives exist. Rather, eventually one must theorize how the two levels integrate together.

---

[8] David L. Miller, *Individualism: Personal Achievement and the Open Society* (Austin: University of Texas Press, 1967), 75.

[9] Musschenga, *The Many Faces of Individualism*, 5.

[10] Kenneth E. Boulding, "General Systems Theory—The Skeleton of Science," *Management Science* 2 (1956): 202–205.

Individualistic Behaviors

One of the difficulties of articulating a simple definition of individualism is that most of the work on the subject empirically describes a "behavioral pattern" and then assigns it to a cultural category. Every human will have to set personal priorities for behavior and values. Much of the research has focused on whether individuals in a given society tend to have personal goals which align with the larger corporate goals, and if they were to have goals either different or disparate from their culture's goals, how would they act upon them.

> Triandis has delineated several defining behavioral attributes of individualistic and collectivist cultures. These could be described as a series of continua:[11]
>
> 1. Dependence: Collectivists tend to define themselves as interdependent on others in the group, whereas individualists tend to define themselves independent of social relationships.
> 2. Goals: "In collectivist cultures, the goals of the group have priority over individual goals and in-group [goals] and individual goals are usually the same; in individualistic cultures, the goals may be different, and if they are in conflict, the individual's goals have priority over the goals of the group."[12]

---

[11] Harry C. Triandis and Michele J. Gelfand, "A Theory of Individualism and Collectivism," in *Handbook of Theories of Social Psychology* (London: Sage Publications, 2012), 506.

[12] Ibid.

3. Behavior: "In collectivist cultures, norms, obligations, and duties guide behavior, whereas in individualist cultures attitudes, personal needs, individual rights, and the contracts the individual has established with others are important determinants of behavior."[13]

4. Relationships: Collectivists are more likely to remain in relationships deemed unsatisfactory, whereas individualists are more likely to leave said groups.

Although informative, these four continua are not properly a definition of individualism; rather they are an empirical description of the behavioral tendency of humans in various societies. Individualism and collectivism, it could be summarized, answer the question of who exists for whom. Do societies exist to serve the needs and augment the existence of the individuals which comprise them, or do individuals have a primary responsibility to preserve the well-being and continuity of the group. While neither side would deny the existence of levels seven and eight of Boulder's model, how the two integrate together is conceived radically differently.

In essence, individualism places the emphasis on the individual. Corporate structures are composed of individuals, and they exist for the individuals which compose them.[14] Therefore, individuals are both able to hold goals or aspirations which do not align with those of the larger corporate entity,

---

[13] Ibid.

[14] "In collectivist cultures, relationships are the figure, and individuals are in the background; in individualistic cultures, individuals are the figure and groups are in the background." Ibid., 508.

and their behavior is not necessarily defined by the wants or norms of the larger group.

Definition of Individualism

For a proper definition of individualism, the underlying cultural axioms must be characterized. Unfortunately, this aspect of individualism has received much less treatment than descriptions of individualistic behavior.[15] However, two axioms should be identified:

1. Selfhood: The individual exists as an independent entity.[16]
2. Individuality: The individual is innately valuable apart from any social constructs they belong to.[17]

In summary, individualism can be defined as the cultural outlook in which the corporate is derived from a collection of individuals, and thus exists because of and for the advancement of these. It is built on the axiom of the independent, innately valuable human individual, and manifests itself in

---

[15] "Individualism has not had the same meaning and application for all who use the word, but it is used in many different senses because often those who use it merely express an emotion or a vaguely formulated attitude without being precise." Miller, *Individualism: Personal Achievement and the Open Society*, 75.

[16] Colin Morris, *The Discovery of the Individual 1050-1200*, 2nd ed. (Toronto: University of Toronto Press, 1987), 1; Robert Bellah, *Habits of the Heart: Individualism and Commitment in American Life* (Berkeley: University of California Press, 1985), 385.

[17] "Individualism is a theory which maintains that selves or persons are the loci of human-value dignity and worth, and that as individuals they constitute the source of new ideas whose practical application is necessary for the growth of society and for the emergence of new values shared by the participants in the group of which the individuals having the new ideas are members." Miller, *Individualism: Personal Achievement and the Open Society*, 75.

individuals who are not internally obligated to think, act, or hold goals in congruence with the larger collection of individuals. The consequence is individuals who are able (or even encouraged) to act or believe disparately from group norms. For the purposes of this paper, this phenomenon will be referred to as *individualism.*

Individualism and Protestant Thought

The demonization of individualism has not been relegated to secular cultural analysts; many Christian thinkers have joined in the fray as well. Interestingly though, almost all of the countries which rank highest on various scales of individualism have been significantly influenced by the Protestant Reformation. Geert Hofstede, Professor Emeritus of Organizational Anthropology at Maastricht University in the Netherlands and founder of the Hofstede Center,[18] has contributed significant effort to measuring several important cultural factors, including individualism. Although his method has received some recent criticism,[19] his basic results are consistent with most other findings, although the ordering may change. The United States (91), Australia (90), Great Britain (89), Canada (80), and the Netherlands (80) score "very high" on Hofstede's Individualism scale—they also all happen to have significant influence from the Protestant

---

[18] The Hofstede Center, headed by Geert Hofsteed operates out of Finland at the time of writing.

[19] Fuan Li and Lerzan Aksoy, "Dimensionality of Individualism–Collectivism and Measurement Equivalence of Triandis and Gelfand's Scale," *Journal of Business and Psychology* 21 (2007): 315.

Reformation.[20] Another international team of scholars, known for the World Values Survey, have tracked changing cultural values for the last few decades. As of 2014, they find Protestant (North Atlantic) Europe, followed closely by English speaking nations (many of which have been influenced by the Protestant Reformation), to be leading the world in self-expression as a cultural value—a value closely tied to individualism.[21] This leads one to question whether, instead of being opposed, there might be some congruence between classic Protestant thought and individualism.

Aims and Methodology

Musschenga muses that "What we observe in most debates about individualism and individualisation is a lack of agreement about, first, the occurrence of certain phenomena; second, their causal connection with individualism and individualisation; and third, their evaluation."[22] The third point will be the express purpose of this paper, namely, to undergo a biblical evaluation of individualism. Is individualism opposed to a biblical worldview, or is there something in Christian, and especially Protestant, thought which supports a nuanced individualism? This paper will not

---

[20] The scale goes from zero to one hundred, with results above eighty being listed as "high." These are followed closely by New Zealand (79), Italy (76), Belgium (75), Denmark (74), Sweden (71), and France (71), most of which also were influenced to one degree or another by the Reformation. Geert Hofstede, *Culture's Consequences: International Differences in Work-Related Values*, Abr. ed. (Newbury Park: Sage, 1984), 158.

[21] All documentation for wave 6 (2010-2014) of their survey can be found at the World Value Survey, http://www.worldvaluessurvey.org/WVSDocumentationWV6.jsp/ (accessed Nov 15, 2015). The WVS groups their finding into cultural groups, "Protestant Europe" and "English Speaking" being two of these groups.

[22] Musschenga, *The Many Faces of Individualism*, 3. For Musschenga, individualization refers roughly to the axioms of individualism: the existence and value of the individual.

include a thorough attempt to define the individual. Rather, it will largely assume for the purpose of this evaluation that an individual is essentially synonymous with a singular human being.

Many Christian thinkers have expressed the concern that Western individualism has misshapen the interpretation of biblical texts. Since the Bible arose in collectivist, agrarian cultures, any reading of it which emphasizes the individual is anachronistic it is claimed.[23] However, despite the collectivist bent of the biblical text, all of the fundamental principles of individualism can be found within it. This casts significant doubt on the claim that reading the text from an individualistic culture distorts the text. Moreover, one actually finds that, although not explicitly addressing individualism, all of the foundational principles of individualism are supported by the Bible. Gary Burnett, noting cases of individuality in the Hellenistic world surrounding the New Testament, notes that

> This is not to claim that the world of the New Testament was anything like our own age in terms of our modern characteristic of individualism. Cohen makes a useful distinction between individualism, individuality and selfhood. Modern Western society is characterised clearly by *individualism*, which can be described as a 'dogmatic posture which privileges the individual over society'. . . . Clearly, it is possible to argue for the importance of selfhood and

[23] "A recurrent charge in recent Pauline scholarship, particularly among those scholars who have been significantly shaped by the application of social-scientific approaches to the ancient world, is that even positing the existence of 'the individual' in Paul depends on an anachronistic projection of modern individualism onto the 'ancient Mediterranean world' and its texts." Ben C. Dunson, "The Individual and Community in Twentieth- and Twenty-First-Century Pauline Scholarship," *Currents in Biblical Research* 9 (2010): 68; Bruce J. Malina, *The New Testament World: Insights from Cultural Anthropology*, 3rd ed. (Louisville: Westminster John Knox Press, 2001), 60-67.

> individuality, whilst recognising that a society in not characterized by individualism.[24]

This paper recognizes along with Burnett that the world of both the Old and New Testaments, while not denying the individual, was not characterized by individualism, as modern Western societies are. However, it will attempt to go one step further than Burnett and demonstrate that, along with supporting selfhood and individuality, the Bible positively evaluates the fundamental principles of individualism, although obviously not directly.

To this end, chapter two will evaluate the two axioms of individualism listed above, which correspond to Cohen's selfhood and individuality. Obviously, if these can be demonstrated to be unsound from a biblical perspective, one should conclude that individualism as an outlook ought to be jettisoned. Few have any qualms with the first axiom, that the individual exists (selfhood). However, many theologians have asserted that the individual is relatively insignificant in the biblical text, and especially in the Old Testament. This chapter will demonstrate that the Bible does uphold the axioms of individualism by presenting the individual as both significant and unique (individuality).

Chapter three will explore the relative value of the individual compared to the corporate to see if an emphasis on it is legitimate. Despite the strong

---

[24] Gary W. Burnett, *Paul and the Salvation of the Individual* (Leiden: Brill, 2001), 29. Burnett cites his categories from Anthony P. Cohen, *Alternative Anthropology of Identity* (New York: Routledge, 1994), 177. Self-hood is defined as self-consciousness, which is the first axiom of individualism. Individuality refers to the uniqueness of each individual, which is a part of the second axiom as will be discussed in chapter 2. This illustrates that one can uphold the axioms of individualism without holding to individualism itself.

corporate elements in both Testaments, the individual is given significant value in the Bible, such that one can reasonably hold to an emphasis on the individual, as individualism demands.

Chapter four will evaluate the autonomy of the individual as a consequence of an individualistic outlook, and question whether this invalidates individualism as a viable system from a biblical perspective. Individualism can easily result in an illegitimate over-emphasis on the freedom of the individual. However, it can be demonstrated philosophically and sociologically that this is not an inevitable outcome of individualism.

Finally, Chapter five will present a summary of the conclusions of the paper and briefly discuss implications.

CHAPTER 2
THE SIGNIFICANCE OF THE INDIVIDUAL

Individuality: The Basis of Individualism

A biblical evaluation of individualism must begin with the basic axioms which individualism assumes. Both politically and socially, individualism understands the individual as the basic unit of society.[1] Any larger group, such as a nation, business, or church congregation, can be fundamentally understood as a collection of individuals. The rights of individuals are basic, and it is the responsibility of larger groups to protect these rights.[2]

Individualism upholds these views because it affirms the axiom of individuality—the idea that individual is significant precisely because each individual is an unique entity, a one-of-a-kind expression of the human race. For this reason, it is important for society to both cherish and nourish the individual. "Individualism holds that at the heart of each person lies a unique core of intuition and feeling that demands creative expression and needs protection against the encroachments both of other individuals and of social institutions."[3]

---

[1] Simon Blackburn, ed., "Individualism," in *The Oxford Dictionary of Philosophy* (Oxford: Oxford University Press, 1994), 191.

[2] James P. Sterba, "Individualism," in *The Cambridge Dictionary of Philosophy*, ed. Robert Audi, 3rd ed. (Cambridge University Press, 1999), 843.

[3] Donald L. Gelpi, ed., *Beyond Individualism: Toward a Retrieval of Moral Discourse in America* (Notre Dame: University of Notre Dame Press, 1989), 2.

The Oxford Dictionary of Philosophy defines an individual as "The things counted as single for the purpose in hand."[4] Individualism defines the human person as the singular unit for any larger group of humans.

> We think of ourselves as people with frontiers, our personalities divided from each other as our bodies visibly are. Whatever ties of love or loyalty may bind us to other people, we are aware that there is an inner being of our own; that we are individuals. To the Western reader it may come as a surprise that there is anything unusual in this experience.[5]

This definition has several interesting features. First, it presents the perspective of society as a collection of individuals, with a distinct ontological boundary between each one. This individual or person is composed of both a physical manifestation (the body) and an inner life. Second, and perhaps most pertinent, is the opinion that this understanding of society is essentially Western in character. The Bible, many will assert, is a thoroughly Oriental book, and thus one might expect its perspective to in some degree be at variance from this understanding.

Biblical Evaluation of Individuality: Methodology

A biblical evaluation of individualism must begin with the axiom of the significance of the individual.[6] This axiom is especially criticized in Old Testament studies, many of which claim not that the individual does not exist *per se*, but rather that is receives so little attention compared to the

---

[4] Blackburn, "Individualism," 191.

[5] Colin Morris, *The Discovery of the Individual 1050-1200*, 2nd ed. (Toronto: University of Toronto Press, 1987), 1.

[6] Since very few would argue against the existence of the individual totally, the first axiom of individualism, selfhood, will not be argued for directly in this chapter, but rather will be included with the second. In other words, if the individual can be proved to be significant in Scripture, it must exist as well.

corporate entity, Israel, that it is of little consequence. However, in the Old Testament one finds surprisingly sophisticated thinking concerning the individual—and not kings and prophets only, but each individual human being. In the New Testament, the significance of the individual comes into even greater focus with a unique contribution to the uniqueness of the individual. Together, these form enough support to uphold the axiom of individuality.[7]

For purposes of argument, this chapter will focus primarily on the evidence from the Old Testament, which as mentioned has typically been assumed to have very little emphasis on the individual. If it can be established that the Old Testament considers each individual—not just kings and prophets—to be significant, despite its considerate collectivist undertones, it would provide a strong argument for the biblical support for the significance of the individual.

Individuals in Ancient Cultures

Before evaluating the significance of the individual, a brief excurses must be made on the role of the individual in Ancient cultures. Ancient cultures are generally considered more prone to collectivism, and since the Bible arose in an Ancient (Eastern) culture, the dominant opinion is that it is a proponent of collectivism as well. Indeed, much of the Biblical text does centers around two important groups: the people of Israel and the Church of Christ. This has led some to conclude that the corporate is the only legitimate entity to receive emphasis in Christian theology:

> God routinely relates to His own people as a collectivity, not as individuals. Under the Old Covenant this collectivity was the nation Israel, and under the New Covenant it is the Church, more

---

[7] The relative value of the individual compared to the corporate will be evaluated in the next chapter.

> often a local church. Nothing of what we say is intended to dismiss individuality, individuation, or God's involvement with individuals. Both testaments testify to the richness of God's relationships with specific people. But although that tends to be the modern Western emphasis, the Scriptures remind us of God's dealings with His group. [8]

However, one should not be too quick to assume that just because the societies into which the Bible was written were more corporately focused than our own, that equates to a Biblically-mandated emphasis on the corporate. Divine revelation into a culture does not necessarily entail an endorsement of it. The culture of the day constitutes important evidence in our understanding of the text, but must not dictate the theological systems that are formed from it.

Moreover, the longstanding assumption that ancient peoples thought very little about the individual has received recent criticism. Speaking about the first century Hellenistic world, Burnett states

> There is considerable unease amongst many classical scholars with the idea of the ancient self as possessing little individuality in any sense that we would recognize. The literature of the period is seen as revealing self-conscious, self-reflecting individuals who were able to take control of their own desires, who demonstrated internal moral and ethical reflection, and, indeed, could often be said to in *individualistic*. (italics original)[9]

The notion that ancient people had little understanding of the individual, nor accounted for it in their cultural thinking is suspect and one that needs revisiting. This casts doubt on the notion that any reading of the Bible

---

[8]Dennis Hiebert and Edmund Neuffeld, "Me and Jesus? Countering Individualism with a More Collectivist Reading of Scripture," (Paper Presented at the 46th Annual Meeting of the Evangelical Theological Scoiety, Chicago, IL, November 17-19, 1994), 12.

[9] Gary W. Burnett, *Paul and the Salvation of the Individual* (Leiden: Brill, 2001), 55.

which emphasizes the individual is anachronistic. The evaluation ought to be made from the biblical evidence itself.

Individuality: A Biblical Evaluation

The Significance of the Individual in the Old Testament

Before one can make any assertion about individualism, they must first confirm whether the individual is a significant entity within the biblical worldview. This might seem aphoristic, but it forms the foundation for all future argument. The Bible uses a host of terms to describe various dimensions of the human being—both physical and spiritual—but the overarching assumption is that these integrate into a cohesive whole, an individual person consisting of a physical body and an inner life. Furthermore, each individual can be distinguished from another, forming its own entity.

Denial of the Significance of the Individual in the Old Testament

There has been a significant strain of scholarship which has asserted that the Old Testament, as an Oriental text, is unconcerned with the individual.[10] The position is summarized by Walther Eichrodt

---

[10] See for instance Ludwig Koehler, *Old Testament Theology*, trans. A.S. Todd (Cambridge: James Clark Co., 1957), 129-30.

> One of the reproaches frequently levelled at Old Testament piety is that it never overcomes its fixation on the collective, but remains stationary at that stage of ancient man's development which rated the value of the individual being inferior to that of the nation; and that it is therefore possible for God to be venerated and worshipped only as the national God, never as the God of the individual.[11]

Bernhard Stade holds to this position, positing that

> In the religion of Israel we are dealing with a relationship not between the individual Israelite (much less the human being) and God, but between the nation Israel and Yahweh. . . . The religious unit is the nation and not the individual. . . . We are a long way from any developed feeling for the individual; the sense of the community is predominant. . . . Even less than the nation can the individual expect to experience Yahweh's help at all times.[12]

This interpretation does not deny the existence of the individual *per se*, but is based on a cultural evolutionary model which asserts that societies must have developed from corporate focus to a more advanced individual focus. Since the Hebrew Scriptures are thoroughly situated in an ancient, Eastern context, they must be unconcerned with the individual, which is a modern, Western construct. However, if it could be shown that the Old Testament does consider the role of the individual in the community and its iteraction with YHWH, it would lend credence to individualism as a possible legitimate worldview.

---

[11] Walther Eichrodt, *Theology of the Old Testament*, trans. J.A. Baker, vol. 2 (Philadelphia: Westminster Press, 1967), 231. Eichrodt cites F. Baumgärtel, R. Smed, and B. Stade as holding this position, which he is arguing against.

[12] Bernhard Stade, *Biblische Theologie* (Tübingen: Mohr Siebeck, 1905), 191, quoted in Eichrodt, *Theology of the Old Testament*, 2:231, note 2.

The Significance of the Individual in Hebrew Thinking

The Old Testament uses a whole host of terms to refer to individual aspects of a human being as synecdoches for the psycho-somatic union which forms an individual human being. This host of terms includes head (רֹאשׁ), face (פָּנֶה), arm (זְרוֹעַ), and blood (דָּם), to name but a few.[13] The Old Testament betrays that Hebrew thought about the individual is actually quite nuanced. It would be curious for authors of the Old Testament to have put so much reflection into the various aspects of an individual if they considered it insignificant. Hebrew thought on the individual also generally follow's Morris' description of the individual as a distinct body with an inner life.[14]

YHWH and the Nephesh

One of the most important pieces of evidence we have for the value of the individual is the term *nephesh* in the Hebrew Psalter. *Nephesh* is a notoriously fluid word, most broadly referring to the throat, and by extension, the breath with comes from it.[15] It is also a common term for the individual person, perhaps with an emphasis on the inner life of that person.[16] Combined with the first person singular pronominal suffix, *naphshi* (נַפְשִׁי) appears eighty-six times throughout the Psalms as a self-referential, roughly equivalent to "I" or "me." Of particular interest are those instances in which the Psalmist entreats YHWH to rise to action on behalf of *naphshi.* "Turn, Oh LORD, and deliver *my life* (*naphshi*); deliver me for the sake of

---

[13] Aubrey Johnson, *The Vitality of the Individual in the Thought of Ancient Israel* (Cardiff: University of Wales Press, 1964). Eichrodt, *Theology of the Old Testament*, 2:131–150.

[14] Colin Morris, *The Discovery of the Individual 1050-1200*, 1.

[15] Ludwig Koehler, et al., *The Hebrew and Aramaic Lexicon of the Old Testament* (Leiden: Brill, 2000), 711-12.

[16] Aubrey Johnson, *The Vitality of the Individual in the Thought of Ancient Israel*, 3–6.

your steadfast love" (Ps 6:4).[17] Interestingly, YHWH's *hesed*, typically associated with His covenantal commitments to the nation, is here entreated to save an individual. Of course, since this Psalm is attributed to David, one could assert that this is appropriate language for David, since as King he has a special relationship to YHWH and the covenant. In other words, YHWH might consider David to be significant as an individual since he is the king, but the same treatment might not be extended to others. However, examples of an individual *nephesh* calling to YHWH for help are not relegated to the Davidic Psalms. Psalm 42, which is attributed to to the Korahites, includes the plea, "Why are you cast down, O *my soul* (*naphshi*) . . . Hope in God; for I shall again praise Him, my help and my God" (Ps 42:11).

Even more interesting are the instances when YHWH is seen interacting directly with the author's soul. YHWH protects David's *nephesh* from going down to Sheol (Ps 16:10, 30:4), restores David's *nephesh* (Ps 23:3), and supports it (54:4). Again, the same themes are found outside of Psalms attributed to David (Ps 49:16).[18] The fact that YHWH interacts with an individual *nephesh* indicates that an individual person is a significant entity in the mind of the biblical authors. YHWH is not merely concerned with the nation, but rather interacts with individuals in similar ways that He interacts with the nation as a whole.

---

[17] All citations are from the New Revised Standard Version (NRSV) unless otherwise noted. Other examples include Ps 17:13, 22:21, 25:20, 26:9, 31:9, to name but a few.

[18] This is an important point. One could argue for the existence of the individual from God's interaction with a number of important biblical figures. However, one could always retort that God only interacts with them in this way because they are theocratic representatives. For a stronger argument, one must show that God has the same concern for each individual, not just kings and prophets.

Similarly, not only did YHWH create the nation of Israel (Is 44:2, Ezek 16:6-8), but He is also involved in the creation of each individual. Most famously, Psalm 139:13 speaks to this, where David claims that YHWH "knit me together in my mother's womb," but again, one must consider whether this was only true of David as a future King of Israel. However, Job too claims that God fashioned him together as by clay (Job 10:9), and The prophet Jeremiah claims the same (Jer 1:5). It is YHWH that brings death and gives life (1 Sam 2:6), and Zechariah 12:1 states that YHWH forms the human spirit within him.

Individuality in the Old Testament

In summary, many scholars have assumed that the Old Testament cannot support individualism, since as an ancient document written in an agrarian society, it by necessity must be unconcerned with the individual, choosing instead to focus on the nation. However, the Old Testament demonstrates a surprising level of sophisticated thinking about the human individual. This is not to say that the Old Testament supports individualism necessarily. It does, however, have a developed enough understanding of the significance of the individual—significant enough for YHWH to interact directly with it—to make this axiom of individualism plausible.

Uniqueness of the Individual

As Donald Gelpi notes, individualism understands the individual to be significant largely because it emphasizes the uniqueness of each individual.[19] Each individual is significant because it is a unique expression of humanity. Since YHWH is personally involved in the formation of each human, one must consider the possibility that He has uniquely created each human

---

[19] Gelpi, *Beyond Individualism: Toward a Retrieval of Moral Discourse in America*, 2

being. If the Bible supports the uniqueness of each individual, it would provide another strong argument for the significance of the individual.

One Church with Many Members

A reasonable place to start is the doctrine of the one church with many members. The church, as a corporate entity, certainly receives a great amount of focus throughout the New Testament epistles. The Body of Christ, the church, is one collective made up of many, distinct members (1 Cor 12:12). Each member receives a unique place within the Body of Christ to serve a unique function. It is so unique that if that person fails to function as part of the body, the whole body suffers (1 Cor 12:18-20).

The uniqueness of each member of the Church stems from a unique role given to each one, defined as a gift (χάρισμα), a service (διακονία), and an activity (ἐνέργημα, 1 Cor 12:4-6). This threefold description forms a multifaceted picture of why each member has a unique function within the Body. The first is clearly supernatural in origin (1 Pet 4:10, 1 Tim 4:14), but the latter two are more likely not, although they are supernaturally sustained. Διακονία probably refers to either a place of service in the body, or perhaps a specially appointed role such as apostle or prophet (1 Tim 4:12).[20] The last word, ἐνέργημα, has a similar connotation, indicating some activity performed based upon ability.

While it is certainly possible to argue that a person only becomes unique once they are made a part of the church, it seems best to conclude that, while each member of the Body is sustained in their ministry by the Holy Spirit (1 Pet 4:11), and while some members receive a special ministry as a gift of the Holy Spirit not based at all upon human ability, the unique

---

[20] William Arndt, Frederick W. Danker, and Walter Bauer, *A Greek-English Lexicon of the New Testament and Other Early Christian Literature* (Chicago: University of Chicago Press, 2000), 230.

function of each member of the Body derives from the innate uniqueness of each individual. These gifts are given to each one individually (1 Cor 12:11, Eph 4:7) to be used by that individual for the common good (12:7). That individual was a unique expression of humanity before their adoption into the body of Christ based on God's unique creative work, and it is on this basis that they are uniquely incorporated into the body as a unique member with a unique function.

The Uniqueness of Each Member of the Trinity

This finding should hardly be surprising, as the body of Christ is modeled on the Trinity itself. This fact has not escaped commentators on 1 Corinthians 12, who as far back as Athanasius[21] have noted the presence of *pneuma, kyrios, and theos* here in rapid succession, indicating a Trinitarian basis for the unity and diversity of the manifestations of the Spirit in the Church.[22] Although, the basic argument of the passage is the unity of the church because of the unity of the Trinity that dispenses gifts and energizes for service, this does not, however, undermine the fact that the ministries are various, just as the essential unity of the Trinity does not undermine the distinction in the persons. Distinctions in the persons of the Trinity are

---

[21] "Knowing this, the blessed Paul does not divide the Triad as you do; but, teaching its unity, when he wrote to the Corinthians concerning things spiritual, he finds the source of all things in one God, the Father, saying 'There are a diversities [sic] of gifts, but the same Spirit. And there are a diversities of ministration, but the same Lord. And there are a diversities of workings, but the same God who worketh all in all.' The gifts which the Spirit divides to each are bestowed from the Father through the Word." *Epistle to Sarapion, I.30*. Quoted from Athanasius, *The Letters of Saint Athanasius Concerning the Holy Spirit*, trans. C.R.B. Shapland (London: Epworth Press, 1951), 142.

[22] Archibald Robertson and Alfred Plummer, *A Critical and Exegetical Commentary on the First Epistle of St Paul to the Corinthians*, International Critical Commentary (Edinburgh: T&T Clark, 1914), 262. Anthony C. Thiselton, *The First Epistle to the Corinthians: A Commentary on the Greek Text*, New International Greek Testament Commentary (Grand Rapids: Eerdmans, 2000), 934-35.

seen through the variety of functions which they perform.[23] In the same way, though the unity of the body is certainly emphasized, that does not negate the reality that, like the Trinity it reflects, the various functions of the distinct members of the body indicates that they are indeed unique, being unique in function. In this way, the singular body of Christ is made up of unique individuals working together to make one body, by which it reflects the Godhead to which she belongs. Although further implications for this mystery will be explored later, it is sufficient to notice that the assumed unity of God's people in Scripture does not obliterate the uniqueness of each member that makes up the whole.

Summary of Biblical Evidence

So far, the argument in favor of individualism is fairly uncontentious. Social scientists generally agree that the human individual exists, a point which finds no difficulty Biblically. The Bible also supports the uniqueness of the individual, as illustrated in our incorporation into the church. This supports the fundamental significance of the individual, a fact which can be demonstrated by God's involvement in creating each human being and his personal involvement in their lives. Even the Old Testament, which some has claimed contains a religion only between Israel and YHWH, shows a significantly nuanced thinking about the individual, and at times does describe its religion in terms of individuals relating to YHWH.

---

[23] "The Father, and the Son, and the Holy Spirit intimate a divine unity of one and the same substance in an indivisible equality; and therefore that they are not three Gods, but one God: although the Father hath begotten the Son, and so He who is the Father is not the Son; and the Son is begotten by the Father, and so He who is the Son is not the Father; and the Holy Spirit is neither the Father nor the Son, but only the Spirit of the Father and of the Son, Himself also co-equal with the Father and the Son, and pertaining to the unity of the Trinity. Yet not that this Trinity was born of the Virgin Mary, and crucified under Pontius Pilate, and buried, and rose again the third day, and ascended into heaven, but only the Son. Nor, again, that this Trinity descended in the form of a dove upon Jesus when He was baptized . . . but only the Holy Spirit. . . . Although the Father, and the Son, and the Holy Spirit, as they are indivisible, so work indivisibly. This is also my faith, since it is the Catholic faith." Augustine, *De Trinitate*, 1.4.7.

Therefore, the Bible does support the two basic axioms of individualism: the existence and significance of the individual. Despite the fact that a large part of the Bible is directly dealing with larger groups of individuals, it clearly has highly developed thinking in this area. Biblically, there is no difficulty asserting that the human individual both exists and is unique, and thus at least the foundation for individualism finds no trouble theologically.

CHAPTER 3

THE INDIVIDUAL AND THE COMMUNITY

The most prevalent behavioral feature of individualism is a preference for individual wants or needs over group concerns.[1] Collectivism as a cultural phenomenon gives a high priority to the goals, customs, and desires of groups to which the individual belongs, either voluntarily or through birth.[2] Individualists are able to opt out of these larger group preferences and act independently.[3]

Individualism as a system is built on the "belief that the individual has a primary reality whereas society is a second-order, derived or artificial construct."[4] If the individual is the building block of society,[5] then the value of the individual is self-derived, and not contingent on the social groups to which they belong.[6] The relative value of the individual compared to the group will be the determining factor on where the emphasis will lie.

---

[1] For a helpful comparison of individualism and collectivism in recent research, see Cigdem Kagıtçıbası, "Individualism and Collectivism," in *Social Behaviors and Application*, vol. 3 of *Handbook of Cross-Cultural Psychology*, ed. John Berry, Marshall Segall, and Cigdem Kagıtçıbası, 2nd ed., (Boston: Allyn and Bacon, 1997), 6-7.

[2] Ibid., 909.

[3] Harry C. Triandis and Michele J. Gelfand, "A Theory of Individualism and Collectivism," in *Handbook of Theories of Social Psychology* (London: Sage Publications, 2012), 506.

[4] Robert Bellah, *Habits of the Heart: Individualism and Commitment in American Life* (Berkeley: University of California Press, 1985), 334.

[5] "The individual—not the community, not public opinion, not external environmental forces—is the source of new ideas that enable society to make changes for the achievement of ideals." David L. Miller, *Individualism: Personal Achievement and the Open Society* (Austin: University of Texas Press, 1967), 3.

[6] Triandis, "A Theory of Individualism and Collectivism," 508.

There are two important considerations for evaluating this central feature of individualism. Although the biblical text supports the significance of the individual, the individual's relationship to the larger communities to which they inevitably belong must be determined. Even if the individual is significant, if this significance is overshadowed by the community, individualism as an ideological system will necessarily collapse. First, one must consider whether the individual has innate value within the broader community, or does it merely function as a spoke in the corporate wheel. Second, one must consider the value of an individual's ability to act independently of their larger in-groups. This chapter will address the former concern, and the later will be the subject of the next chapter.

Collectivism in the Bible

As discussed in the previous chapter, much of the Bible focuses on two corporate groups, Israel and the church of Christ. This gives the Bible a decidedly corporate focus. This feature is further augmented by the covenantal nature of these relationships, which binds those in them together as a corporate entity.

This corporate focus is especially true for Israel, which was bound together as a nation by the Mosaic Law. Ancient law codes were first written to delimit the place of the individual within the larger community. The Law of Hammurabi, for instance, is decidedly collectivist, providing sanctions on individuals who disturb the greater peace, and generally presumes that each individual is responsible for the maintenance of the well-being of the group.[7] The concept of individual rights is often considered to have developed late within legal systems, first being seen prominently in Greece and Rome in the 3rd century BCE.[8] Having much more affinity geographically, linguistically, and chronologically to Hammurabi than to Athens, one might expect the Mosaic Law to be decidedly collectivist in tone.

---

[7] Ibid., 499.

[8] Ibid., 500.

The assumption then has largely been that the Old Testament elevates the collective over the individual.[9] Old Testament scholar Joel Kaminsky states that the "individual's very self-understanding was derived from his or her relationship to the community."[10] This is contrary to the view of individualism, which sees the individual's value as self-derived. Although the individual does come sharper into focus in the New Testament, it too spends a significant amount of time discussing the individual's relationship to the church.

Despite the significant amount of emphasis in both Testaments on corporate structures and relationships, one should not be too quick to accept the notion that an individual's value is only derived from their place in the community. Rather, the individual has a primary place in the doctrine of sin and future eschatology—two of the most important biblical doctrines.

Individuals and Responsibility for Sin

Corporate Punishment for Sin

Cases of corporate punishment for individual sins are profoundly uncomfortable for both Old Testament scholars and readers alike. The sin of Achan (Josh 7) provides an illustrative case of corporate punishment. The author is quite explicit that it was Achan, an individual, that broke the ban which had been placed on all the plunder from Jericho (Josh 6:21). However, despite the fact that only one man broke the ban, it is said that the sons of Israel (בְּנֵי־יִשְׂרָאֵל) transgressed the ban. Consequently, YHWH was angry against the entire group, so much so that when the army of Israel went up to attack Ai, they were defeated.

---

[9] Osterley and Robinson provide an excellent example of this strain of scholarship, saying "In the older view, the human unit was not the individual but the community." W.O.E. Osterley and Theodore H. Robinson, *An Introduction to the Books of the Old Testament* (London: Society for Promoting Christian Knowledge, 1961), 311.

[10] Joel S. Kaminsky, *Corporate Responsibility in the Hebrew Bible*, vol. 196 of *Journal for the Study of the Old Testament Supplemental Series*, (Sheffield: Sheffield Academic Press, 1995), 153.

Any reasonable reader might wonder why YHWH would see fit to punish thirty-six men who fell in battle, along with their families, for a sin which they did not personally commit. Should this not be seen as undeniable proof that the Old Testament is not concerned with individuals, but rather only corporate groups, since the punishment for breaking the ban was initially leveled not against the individual who committed the sin? This case of corporate punishment for a personal sin is no isolated incident. There are cases of families being included in the punishment for sins, such as the rebellion of Korah (Num 16:1-50) or the leprosy of Naaman (2 Kgs 5:27).

Kaminsky has done excellent work in the area of what he terms "trans-generational corporate retribution,"[11] and correctly notes that it is the covenant framework of the Old Testament that is fundamental to understanding this concept. The majority of the Hebrew Scriptures—and some might argue all of it—is focused on the people of God, the nation of Israel, that has bound themselves to God and each other through covenant. Because of this, it should not be surprising that an individual's actions have further ramifications. "The prevalence, centrality and persistence of the corporate idea becomes much more understandable once one realizes that these ideas flow out of the covenantal theology that is so important to the whole structure and ideology of the deuteronomistic history."[12] Because of the covenantal framework, one might expect consequences for actions to extend to the larger group. This does not necessarily mean that the individual is somehow not important because of this.

This particular component of the Old Testament becomes even more pronounced during the period of the monarchy. The king of Israel or Judah becomes the representative of the nation,[13] and blessing and curses flow to the nation based upon his actions. Kaminsky notes a particularly interesting example in Manasseh, whose rule over Judah is described in 2 Kings 21. Like many of the kings before him, he "did what was evil in the sight of the LORD" (2 Kgs 21:2). He misled Israel into becoming even more wicked

---

[11] Joel S. Kaminsky, *Corporate Responsibility in the Hebrew Bible*, 44.

[12] Ibid., 54. Kaminsky here is arguing from the assumption of a deuteronomistic redactor to the Hebrew Scriptures—a position which this author finds unconvincing—but which certainly could be extended to the entirety of the Old Testament.

[13] Ibid., 37.

than the surrounding nations (2 Kgs 21:9)—a resounding criticism indeed. Because of the sins of Manasseh, YHWH pronounced impending judgment upon Jerusalem. This case study provides an interesting example, as both Manasseh and the people of Israel are held responsible for the sin of the nation, Manasseh for instigating and the people for following. Because of this, Kaminsky claims, the guilt for Manasseh's actions are transferred to the nation as a whole. "These passages [2 Kgs 23:31-36, 24:8-17]," Kaminsky states, "not only reveal that the deuteronomistic historian employs the idea of intra-generational retribution in his attempt to explain the eventual downfall of both the North and the South, but additionally they provide support for the existence of another type of corporate thinking in which sins transfer across generations." However, perhaps it is best to not say that the guilt for Manasseh's actions were transferred to the nation, but rather that this singular person provides a snapshot of the sinfulness of the nation. As noted above, the nation is not judged solely because of the sinfulness of her king. Rather, the evil royal lineage mirrors the state of the nation. Kaminsky himself, despite disagreeing on some details, seems to hold this conclusion, stating that "the party who received the punishment did act wickedly, but nevertheless received the punishment which had been building for several generations."[14]

The pattern in the Hebrew Scriptures is that punishment might come on corporate groups such as families or generations for sins which they did not specifically commit, however, those punishments were the result of disobedience which had been accumulating. It is not the case that YHWH decided to punish others who were innocent because there is no concept of the individual. Rather, one must bear in mind that the covenant affects how guilt and punishment works within the Old Testament. The covenant which binds the nation together includes the possibility that those who did not commit the sin personally might receive some of the consequences of that sin. This is especially true in cases of the sin of theocratic representatives such as the king.

Individual Responsibility for Sin

Although there are cases of corporate consequences for sin, it is the individual which is ultimately held responsible for their actions. Nowhere is

---

[14] Ibid., 44.

the responsibility of the individual sinner more clearly seen than in Deuteronomy 24:16, a passage tightly paralleled by Jeremiah 31:29-30 and Ezekiel 18:20. Deuteronomy is unmistakably purposed to provide a code of conduct and standard of norms for a community. In this regard, it is extremely consistent with other ancient Near Eastern law codes. However, it has an individualistic approach to dealing with sin.

The Mosaic Law is quite clear at this point that there is an individual consequence for the sinner, one which must not be transferred to another person, parent or child. Indeed, the entire picture of Deuteronomy is that, despite making a corporate covenant, each individual had the responsibility to abide by it. Although the Old Testament does not shy away from corporate consequences for sin (Deut 28:15), judgement is always leveled on the basis of personal actions.

Eugene Merrill, commenting on this feature of Deuteronomy, asserts that

> The supreme worth of the individual (as well as his responsibility before God) is seen in his accountability as a sinner. The notion of Israel as a community, as almost a corporate personality, was pervasive throughout the Old Testament but never at the expense of the solitary person. Admittedly, the emphasis on the individual's personal standing before God is more highly developed in later Old Testament revelation.[15]

Many Old Testament scholars are uncomfortable with this emphasis in Deuteronomy, preferring instead to account for it as a late redaction, since it has a greater emphasis on the individual.[16] However, the linear progression from corporate focus to individualism must be set aside as an incomplete model. Burnett argues this point emphatically:

> Non-modern, non-Western societies, whether modern day or primitive, or the Classical, or Hellenistic worlds, are often characterized in this way, with little regard given to the power of

---

[15] Eugene H. Merrill, *Deuteronomy*, The New American Commentary (Nashville: Broadman & Holman Publishers, 1994), 322–323.

[16] T. H. Robinson, *An Introduction to the Books of the Old Testament*, 43–45.

> self-conscious individuals acting within their own worlds. The essence of the human beings who lived in these ancient societies was the thinking self, their own self-conscious beings, which were active in forming and changing the cultural in their own day. We may well recognize very distinct differences between their worlds and our own, but we cannot deny to these people thinking self-conscious.[17]

As cultural anthropologists come to terms with individuality in the ancient world, the opinion that Deuteronomy must have been written later because the role that it gives the individual becomes less defensible. However, there is no good reason for this interpretive move. Instead,

> The Hebrew Scriptures should not be seen as either to ignore the importance of the individual, or to continue a pattern of progression from corporatism to individualism. There is, in fact, a more nuanced theology of individual and community, whereby an individual's actions and relationship to God is important, but only in so far as they are part of a larger narrative framework of the community as a whole.[18]

Although consequences for sin might extend to others because of the broader covenant framework of the Old Testament, judgement for sin is always wrought on the personal actions of the individual. This is perhaps the greatest statement on the value of the individual in the whole Old Testament.

If this theme is present in the Old Testament, it is seen all the more clearly in the New Testament. One example is found in Jesus' parable of the talents, found in Luke 19:11-27 and Matthew 25:14-30. In the parable, when the master returns and demands an account from each slave as to how they used his money, he calls each to judgement individually, and judges each one based upon how they personally invested his money. It was not enough for the last slave that the first had invested wisely. He was judged for how he individually had been a steward. Interestingly, this parable extends

---

[17] Gary W. Burnett, *Paul and the Salvation of the Individual* (Leiden: Brill, 2001), 28.

[18] Ibid., 77.

individual judgment beyond punishment for sin to reward for righteousness (1 Cor 3:13-15).

Salvation and the Individual

The Individual in Pauline Scholarship

In the mid-20th century, a theological debate was raging between Rudolf Bultmann and his student Ernst Käsemann. These two scholars had taken note of the individual and corporate undertones in the New Testament, but had settled on different emphases. Bultmann underscored the role of the individual in the salvation process, arguing from Pauline anthropological terms. Bultmann does not ignore the community in his treatment of Paul. Rather, "while the individual serves as the starting point and most prominent focus of Bultmann's concern, the extra-personal life of the community of faith is never ignored. Paul's kerygma does individualize, but it also transforms one's self-understanding towards care for the community."[19] However, in the end, each person stands before God as an individual. Käsemann took exception to this stance, feeling that "Bultmann's preoccupation with the individual and 'existential decision' led him to neglect dominant, communally-focused themes in Paul's letters."[20] Thus, although both recognized the presence of the individual and communities in the salvation process, they could not agree on where the emphasis should lie.

This debate has not been totally resolved. In recent Pauline scholarship, there has been a noticeable shift in focus from the salvation of the individual to the salvation of people groups.[21] Scholars such as E.P. Sanders have drawn attention to the tension in ethnic people groups in the time period of the writing of the New Testament, and have suggested that much of the New Testament is actually about who is and can be saved, instead of the classic Protestant interpretation of how an individual can come into

---

[19] Ben C. Dunson, "The Individual and Community in Twentieth- and Twenty-First-Century Pauline Scholarship," *Currents in Biblical Research* 9 (2010): 66.

[20] Ibid., 68.

[21] Gary W. Burnett, *Paul and the Salvation of the Individual*, 1–5.

right standing before God. The merit of these scholars' arguments is outside the scope of this work, but it has certainly fueled sentiments among New Testament scholars that perhaps we have distorted the New Testament to be more individualistic than it truly is. Dr. Robert Jewett in his work on Romans contends that

> Paying careful attention to Paul's gospel in the context of the Roman imperial propaganda of the time prevents the modern reader from imposing the individualism of the dominant Western 'theological tradition' of reading Romans onto Paul's letters. Instead, we must understand that the 'primary scope' of Paul's language of salvation was 'the group . . . rather than the individual', although Jewett concedes that the individual was not wholly neglected.[22]

Jewett's position amounts to a rejection of individualism as an emphasis on the individual instead of the corporate as a legitimate way to read Pauline theology.

The Individual in Classic Protestant Thought

Perhaps no text demonstrates the effect of the social science on exegesis (and why a study such as this is paramount) than Rom 1:16-17, reasonably the most influential verse in the last five hundred years of Western history. The center of Luther's so-called Reformation discovery, the interpretation of this text by the Reformers was distinctly individualistic. Luther describes his experience meditating on the text as follows:

---

[22] As summarized in Ben C. Dunson, "The Individual and Community in Twentieth- and Twenty-First-Century Pauline Scholarship," 69.

> At last, by the mercy of God, meditating day and night, I gave heed to the context of the words, namely, 'In it [the Gospel] the righteousness of God is revealed.'. . . There I began to understand that the righteousness of God is . . . the passive righteousness with which a merciful God justifies us by faith. Here I felt that I was altogether born again and had entered paradise itself through open gates . . . thus that place in Paul [Rom 1:16-17] was for me truly the gate of paradise.[23]

Luther understood Romans 1:16-17 to be talking about the means of the salvation of the individual. Recent scholarship wants to define the gospel as espoused by Romans 1:16-17 as addressing not the salvation of individuals but the reconciliation of conflict between ethnic groups or cosmic forces.[24]

However, modern readers of Paul should not be so quick to dismiss more individualistic readings of Paul as Western inventions based upon the previous discussion on the centrality of the individual in judgement for both sin and righteousness, strains of individuality in the ancient world, and the overall value of the individual throughout the Bible. This "alerts us to the possibility that the collective issues in the gospel which Paul introduces un in vv. 16 and 17 are not the whole story."[25]

Personal and Group Eschatology

The interplay between the group and the individual in the New Testament is nowhere seen clearer than in the eschatology of the New Testament, which both builds on the Old Testament themes previously mentioned and further develops them. New Testament eschatology has many dimensions which are decidedly corporate in focus. This is hardly surprising, considering the church, a corporate entity, receives so much emphasis throughout the New Testament books of all genres.

---

[23] Martin Luther, "Preface to the Complete Edition of Luther's Latin Writings," in *Luther's Works*, ed. Helmut Lehmann, trans. Lewis W. Spitz, American ed. (Philadelphia: Muhlenberg Press, 1960), 34:337.

[24] Gary W. Burnett, *Paul and the Salvation of the Individual*, 137.

[25] Ibid., 138.

In many passages, the New Testament portrays a singular people of God who share a common interest and a common destiny. The church has been born together—as one entity—because of the resurrection of Christ into one common inheritance (1 Pet 1:3-4). This future inheritance has very clearly been given to the church as a unit. Presumably, every individual who a member of the church invisible is thus privy to this inheritance (1 John 5:1). Although this is true, the eschatological emphasis is clearly corporate, as the church as a whole shares a common hope. The church as a whole groans together, waiting for the consummation of her adoption (Rom 8:23). As a whole we wait in patience for the glorious future promised to us (Rom 8:25). Together we are being built up into a spiritual house (1 Pet 2:5), a holy temple and dwelling place for God (Eph 6:21-22). We will all be changed into our new glorified bodies (1 Cor 15:51). These few examples are sufficient to make the point. The church, because of her common adoption through union with Christ, shares a common hope.

This common future eschatology is given to the church corporately. Additionally, each Christian, it is assumed, must be a part of the church—no one is allowed to voluntarily refuse admittance. If you are a part of the church, *ipso facto* you share the common hope of its glorious future in Christ. This fact is enough for many theologians to declare the case closed against individualism. Surely, since the New Testament places such a great emphasis on the corporate nature of the church, there is no place for an emphasis on the individual.

On the contrary, it is not true that the New Testament is devoid of a focus on the individual, even within its eschatology. As noted previously, judgement for sin and reward for righteousness has a decidedly personal emphasis in both Testaments. Each human being is destined to stand before the Judgement Seat of Christ to receive recompense for their actions (1 Cor 3:13-15, 2 Cor 5:10). The particular construction of πάντας ἡμᾶς (all of us) leaves out no human. This perhaps makes sense for those who are outside of the church, who will be judged based upon their rejection of Christ (Rev 20:11-15). However, how does one reconcile that each person within the church will be personally judged but yet is guaranteed a common future because of their position as a member of the corporate body the church?

For our purposes, the salient feature of New Testament eschatology is that while each member of the church has come to share in a common hope, a common destiny, and a common inheritance; each individual will be evaluated by God before sharing in it. It is not a group evaluation—indeed the final destiny of the group appears unchangeable. The bride of Christ will be adorned and made ready when the Son comes to inherit His kingdom (Rev 19:7). However, how each person contributes is a matter of individual concern. Thus, eschatologically, each dimension can be seen. The church is a corporate entity that shares a cooperate destiny. However, the final evaluation will be individual in nature, and thus the command to the church must be for each individual to make herself ready.

The Protestant doctrine of the priesthood of all believers is the lynchpin by which these two truths can be held together. A central tenant of the Protestant Reformation, and yet one that is often misrepresented,[26] the priesthood of all believers holds together the focus on the community in the New Testament, but also recognizes the special status of each believer within the larger framework of the church.

> Luther's doctrine of the priesthood of all believers was, first, Christ-centered, with each individual believer deriving his status as a priest from his union to Christ through faith alone. Second, Luther's doctrine was community-centered, with each believer serving as a priest to other believers, helping them draw near to God and maintain justifying faith throughout life.[27]

The priesthood of all believers is founded upon each believer's union with Christ. This individual union is formed by each individual's personal response to Christ. The individual evaluation of each person is the greatest statement of their value before God. The fact that each person is evaluated for their own sin is a ringing endorsement for the value of each individual from a Biblical understanding. It is not sufficient to merely say that both the corporate and the individual is seen in the New Testament. Rather, it is better to say that that which is primarily individual has received corporate dimension based upon the covenant connection of God's people.

---

[26] Timothy George, *The Theology of the Reformers* (Nashville: Broadman & Holman, 1988), 95.

[27] Mark Rogers, "A Dangerous Idea? Martin Luther, E.Y. Mullins, and the Priesthood of All Believers," *Westminster Theological Journal* 72 (2010): 123.

The Individual's Role in Salvation

Throughout the Pauline epistles, the faith of the individual takes center stage as the means of appropriating the salvation which is offered by the gospel. Paul makes clear links between placing one's faith in the work of Christ and the subsequent salvation both the individual and the new group to which he or she belongs obtains. Romans 10:9-17 is one text where this link is seen, for "a person believes" which results in their salvation. Brian Dodd argues that despite the conclusion one reaches on the precise meaning of faith (πίστις) in the book of Romans, "the point is indisputable that Paul does indeed conceive of the believer putting faith in Christ."[28]

Outside of Paul, individual faith is presented as a necessary prerequisite for salvation. Peter declares to Cornelius that "in every nation anyone who fears Him and does what is right is acceptable to Him. . . . All the prophets testify about [Christ] that everyone who believes in Him receives forgiveness of sins through His name" (Acts 10:35, 43). Salvation here is not being offered to a people group; even an isolated individualis given the call to believe in Christ. Interestingly, Peter sees this as consistent with God's actions in the Old Testament as well. Hebrews 11:6 states that anyone who wishes to please God must have faith, and John 3:16 famously declares "that everyone who believes in him may not perish but may have eternal life."

This should hardly be surprising: if eschatological judgment is to be personal in nature, one might expect a positive conclusion to that judgement to be based on some personal action as well. This is not to downplay the significant role that the corporate people of God holds in the discussion, but raises the question of whether recent scholarship has become unbalanced in its criticism. It is true that the gospel, as understood not just by Paul but by all of the New Testament authors, has significant implications for people groups. It is also true that, eschatologically, the final destiny of each person is largely based on which group to which they are apart. However, we would do great disservice to the theology of the New Testament if we disregard the basic truism that a person is placed into the

---

[28] Brian Dodd, "Romans 1:17—A Crux Interpretum for the ΠΙΣΤΙΣ ΧΡΙΣΤΟΥ Debate," *Journal of Biblical Literature* 113 (1994): 472.

people of God through a personal act of faith. Thus without the individual and his act of faith, there is no corporate of which to speak.

Summary of Biblical Evidence

Even if the individual does exist and has some significance from a biblical perspective as confirmed in the previous chapter, it would not lead to individualism if the individual lacks relative value compared to the corporate. However, it is quite reasonable to assert that the individual finds an important place within a well-formed theological system. The personal responsibility levied on each person for their sin is perhaps the greatest testament to this value. The role of the individual in their final destiny, namely the act of faith and centrality of the individual in eschatological judgement, confirms this notion. The individual clearly both exists and is valuable.

With this established, one must ask the pertinent question for evaluating individualism: is an emphasis on the individual instead of the collective an appropriate one given the biblical evidence? First, it must be restated that recent attempts to purge classical Protestantism of an emphasis on the individual based on supposed misrepresentation of the Biblical texts must be considered overdrawn.

When one considers the immense value placed on the individual human being throughout Scripture, it becomes difficult to argue that emphasizing the individual over the corporate is entirely inappropriate. It is not sufficient to merely say that both the corporate and the individual is seen in the Bible. Rather, it is better to say that that which is primarily individual by nature has received corporate dimension based upon the covenant connection of God's people. Thus one should expect that the actions of individuals has further ramifications for the corporate body. This, however, does not imply that an emphasis on the individual is inappropriate, although it does render it impossible to conceive of the individual entirely apart from these constructs. It is thus legitimate biblically to construe the corporate entities of Scripture as built upon the individuals which make them up without misrepresenting Scripture.

CHAPTER 4

AUTONOMY AND INDIVIDUALISM

Individualism and Autonomy

The central question in a biblical evaluation of individualism is how to understand autonomy. Individualism to one degree or another implies autonomy of the individual, although how that exactly is defined is a matter of debate.

Autonomy as Self-Containment

For some, autonomy is nothing more than the self-containment of each individual. Miller comments that "Only human beings have selves and are persons. The basic requirement for being a self is that a person (or a self) be an object to itself; a self must be able to conceive of itself, to 'look' at itself as it looks at objects. It must be self-conscious."[1] In Miller's definition, humanity is partitioned into distinct units of individual human beings. In this sense of autonomy, individuals are independent in that they do not derive their existence from one another. It does not imply that individuals are free from influence from other individuals, nor that they should be. Rather, it merely proposes that the individual should be understood as the basic unit of society because it is the smallest unit which can conceive of itself as an individual "object."

Autonomy as Self-Direction

Others conceive of personal autonomy in a more comprehensive manner. De Tocqueville laments that "Individualism is a mature and calm feeling, which disposes each member of the community to serve himself rather than the mass of his fellow-creatures; and to draw apart from his families and friends; so that, after he has formed a little circle of his own, he willingly

---

[1] David L. Miller, *Individualism: Personal Achievement and the Open Society* (Austin: University of Texas Press, 1967), 15.

leaves society at large to itself."[2] His critique is all too clear: once the emphasis shifts from the corporate body to the individual, it is inevitable that the individual will cease to care about all others in the society, save perhaps a select few of one's own choosing. The individual is autonomous in that it is self-directed; it forms its own priorities and mandates its own actions, if necessary without regard to the other individuals around him. "The utilitarian [self-directing] individualist views human life as the individual pursuit of power in a world of threatening competitors. Utilitarian individualists expect the social contracts they make to advance their interests by protecting and increasing personal wealth and influence."[3] This opinion is precisely the reason why individualism has had so much criticism levied against it by both social and religious critics.

Immanuel Kant and Moral Self-Governance

John Macken summarizes the development of the term autonomy as follows:

> [Autonomy appears] in German jurisprudence after the Reformation, first in a negative sense in the Catholic polemic against the Reformation, as implying anarchy. As both Protestant and Catholic jurists turned to natural law to solve the problem posed by their inability to find consensus on an explicitly Christian basis, 'autonomy' is used in a positive sense and with time is used of the right of individuals or corporations to run their own affairs within the limits of the larger framework set by the law.[4]

Individual autonomy developed as a philosophical answer for post-Reformation Europe's dilemma of how to proceed without a singular religious authority to bind society together. Since Europe was no longer united religiously, many sought to ground morality on "natural law," or

---

[2] Alexis de Tocqueville, *Democracy in America*, trans. Henry Reeve, vol. 2 (New York: J & H. G. Langley, 1840), 584.

[3] Donald L. Gelpi, ed., *Beyond Individualism: Toward a Retrieval of Moral Discourse in America* (Notre Dame: University of Notre Dame Press, 1989), 1–2.

[4] John Macken, *The Autonomy Theme in the Church Dogmatics* (Cambridge: Cambridge University Press, 1990), 3.

some shared aspect of humanity that transcended the Catholic-Protestant distinction.

Eighteenth century German philosopher Immanuel Kant made significant contributions to this field, permanently shaping much of Western thinking. Kant spoke of autonomy as the freedom of the individual to make personal moral distinctions. Kant's categorical imperative supposed that ethical decisions are fundamentally grounded in the will of the individual:

> At the core of the moral philosophy of Immanuel Kant is the claim that morality centers on a law that human beings impose on themselves, necessarily providing themselves, in doing so, with a motive to obey. Kant speaks of agents who are morally self-governed in this way as autonomous.[5]

Kant sought to ground morality within the individual instead of an outside authority. It was not so far an extension to claim then that each individual can ultimately choose their own ethical directives autonomously, or in complete isolation from other members of society, and in fact this is the direction much of Western thinking has developed.[6] In this strain of individualism, each individual becomes self-directing, making personal decisions based solely upon personal values and inclinations. In order to distinguish these two definitions of personal autonomy, the later will be referred to as *Libertarian Individualism.*

Biblical Evaluation of Libertarian Individualism

Even a cursory perusal of the biblical data appears to render Libertarian Individualism fundamentally flawed from a biblical perspective. The individual human being, despite having the freedom to act according to their own will (Josh 24:15), is, biblically speaking, most certainly not free to make personal choices on the nature of morality. "Each man doing what is right in his own eyes," a maxim for complete personal autonomy in the

---

[5] Jerome B. Schneewind, *The Invention of Autonomy: A History of Modern Moral Philosophy* (Cambridge: Cambridge University Press, 1997), 483.

[6] For an argument that this is the inevitable result of individualism, Cf. Gelpi, *Beyond Individualism: Toward a Retrieval of Moral Discourse in America*, 3.

Libertarian sense, is the sweeping condemnation of the entire Judges period in which the fledgling Israelite nation hardly flourished (Judg 21:25, also Deut 12:8). It is the wicked (Ps 12:4) and the fool (Prov 3:5) who acknowledges no other source for direction than himself. Libertarian Individualism is also at odds with the basic principle of humble Christlikeness which is to be the model of the church's members dealings with each other (Phil 2:2-8). A Kantian view of autonomy is an illegitimate application of individualism, and thus any system which naturally or necessarily leads to Libertarian Individualism must be considered suspect from a Biblical perspective.

Sola Scriptura and Libertarian Individualism

It has been noted that cultures significantly influenced by the Protestant Reformation have a tendency to support individualism. If Protestant doctrine were shown to lend itself to a Libertarian mode of thinking, it could prove troublesome for Protestant theologians.

The final evaluation of this phenomenon might well rest in the evaluation of the Protestant doctrine of *sola scriptura*. Catholic theologian Brad Gregory provides a thorough argument for the connection between modern pluralism and the Protestant doctrine of *sola scriptura*. Despite its diversity of opinion, Gregory claims that "Western Christianity on the eve of the Reformation comprised an institutional worldview."[7] This institutional worldview was shattered, however, when the Reformers rejected not just the current moral state of the Roman Church, but the entire institution as a "perverted form of Christianity."[8] Lacking an institution on which to rest its truth claims, the Reformers turned to Scripture alone as the basis for Christian doctrine.[9] The problem, Gregory asserts, is that from the

---

[7] Brad S. Gregory, *The Unintended Reformation: How a Religious Revolution Secularized Society* (Cambridge: Belknap Press, 2012), 82–83.

[8] Ibid., 86.

[9] "No cause imaginable could avert our will from giving the function of supreme and sole judge to holy writ. . . .We acknowledge Holy Scripture to be a most perfect rule." William Chillingsworth, *The Religion of the Protestants: A Safe Way to Salvation* (Oxford: Leonard Lichfield, 1638), 42. "By the 'religion of the protestants' I do not understand the doctrine of Luther, or Calvin, or Melanchthon; nor the confession of Augusta, or Geneva, nor the

beginning of the Reformation, Christians differed on the exact meaning of Scripture.[10] This "individualistic, hermeneutical anarchy"[11] could have but one result—an inevitable plunge into individualistic hyperpluralism,[12] or Libertarian Individualism.

Although there are several problems with Gregory's argument,[13] his basic premise is compelling. After the invention of the printing press and the translation of the Scripture into the vernacular, reading Scripture could become a private, individual affair. If the interpretive authority was removed from an institution and placed instead in the hands of Scripture (wielded by the individual reader), it seems inevitable that naught but a plurality of readings would follow. Without an overarching institution to maintain catholicity, it would seem that *sola scriptura* has no possible result but Libertarian Individualism. If this is true, then any reading of Scripture which emphasizes the individual must be rejected because of the conclusion to which it leads. This would amount to nothing less than a necessary total

---

Catechism of Heidelberg, nor the Articles of the Church of England, no, nor the harmony of protestant confessions; but that wherein they all agree, and which they all subscribe with a greater harmony, as a perfect rule of their faith and actions; that is, the Bible. The Bible, I say, the Bible only, is the religion of the protestants! Whatsoever else they believe besides it, and the plain, irrefragable, indubitable consequences of it, well may they hold it as a matter of opinion; but as a matter of faith and religion, neither can they with coherence to their own grounds believe it themselves, nor require the belief of it of others. . . .I, for my part. . .do profess plainly that I cannot find any rest for the sole of my foot but upon this rock only." Ibid., 375–76.

[10] "It is thus misleading to say that 'Protestantism itself splintered into rival denominations or 'confessions,' as If there was some point in the early Reformation when anti-Roman Christians had agreed among themselves about what scripture said and God taught. There wasn't." Gregory, *The Unintended Reformation*, 91.

[11] Ibid., 95.

[12] Ibid., 92.

[13] Although Gregory acknowledges diversity in medieval Latin Christianity, he still conceives of it as essentially a singular institution. In Gregory's view, the singular institution of the Catholic church provided the West with a singular worldview. Thus the church acted as the dam against the impending deluge of religious and moral pluralism. Once Protestantism rejected "the institution" in favor of *sola scriptura*, the unity of the church was cracked, and the dam would inevitably break, flooding Western civilization in pluralism. Gregory, however, envisions medieval Latin Christianity as too monolithic, thus casting doubt on this conclusion. Calling pre-Trent Medieval Western Christianity a singular (unified) entity seems ambitious at best.

rejection of individualism by the Christian, and would reflect poorly on Protestant thinking in general.

The Individual and the Hermeneutical Process

Libertarian Individualism is at odds with Scripture itself and its understanding of the role of the individual in the hermeneutical process. The Apostle Peter instructs that Scripture did not arise from the will of the individual prophet (1 Pet. 1:20).[14] The writers of Scripture were not simply giving private moral maxims, but rather, as their spirits communed with the Spirit of God, they wrote that which had come from God Himself. It is exactly this basis on which the authority of Scripture is built, that it comes not from human opinion, but is the Word of God. Paul describes this process as "God-breathing" (θεόπνευστος), and it is on this basis that Scripture is "useful for teaching, for reproof, for correction, and for training in righteousness" (2 Tim 3:16). The result of the proper use of the Scriptures is that each believer might be rendered capable and equipped for good works (3:17). This process is significant for this discussion, for it shows an interplay between an individual and an outside source of authority.

It would appear that the Protestant emphasis on Scripture is hardly misplaced, but the question arises as to how Scripture itself envisions its use by the individual. The description ὁ τοῦ θεοῦ ἄνθρωπος (the person of God) indicates that the Scripture has effective force for each person, and not just the church as an institution. At the same time though, Paul also instructs Timothy to give attention to the public reading of Scripture (1 Tim 4:13), an activity which undoubtedly took place within the church. It seems then that the Scriptures take on life for the individual believer precisely

---

[14] The statement ἰδίας ἐπιλύσεως οὐ γίνεται is probably not speaking against a private interpretation of prophetic revelation contra many translations of the verse, starting with the KJV. ἐπιλύσεως is a hapax legomenon, and has typically been understood to mean "interpretation." However, the word in general means a discharge or a release from. Cf. Aeschylus, *Seven Against Thebes* 134. It can be used metaphorically though for something which is "discharged" from a person, such as a spell. James Moulton and George Milligan, *The Vocabulary of the Greek Testament* (London: Hodder and Stoughton, 1930), 242. Thus it is probably best to translate the phrase "did not find its origin from inside of the prophet." In other words, the prophet did not simply write whatever he wanted and call it a "prophetic word."

within the context of the corporate body of Christ. They neither arose from nor belong wholly to the individual, but rather is God's gift to His people, both corporately and individually.

One again sees in the doctrine of Scripture itself the very principles which necessitates a rejection of Libertarian Individualism. Private interpretation of Scripture—that which conforms to naught but the individuals own will—is by no means a legitimate use of Scripture, for Scripture, though useful for the individual, is meant for use also by the corporate. This is not to deny the significant use of the Scriptures which may be personally appropriated. However, the dominant example of Scripture is the Word of God read amongst the corporate body (Neh 8:1-4, 2 Kgs 23:2, Deut 31:11, 2 Chr 17:9, Acts 15:21).

This casts doubt on Gregory's premise that *sola scriptura* necessitates a spiral into Libertarian Individualism. For certain, a plethora of interpretations of Holy Scripture have existed, even in the days of Jesus (Mk 12:18). However, the very doctrine of *sola scriptura*, if properly applied, ought to safeguard some form of catholicity, for each interpreter has vowed to place Scripture first over personal preference as the interpretive norm. Lewis Sperry Chafer makes this express point

> It is exceedingly easy to twist or mold the Word of God to make it conform to one's preconceived notions. To do this is no less than 'handling the word of God deceitfully' (2 Cor. 4:2), and is worthy of judgment from Him whose Word is thus perverted. At no point may the conscience be more exercised and the mind of God more sought than when delving into the precise meaning of the Scriptures and when giving those findings to others.[15]

Individualism and the Subjection of the Individual

The moral, ethical, or interpretive self-directing individual must be rejected from a biblical standpoint. However, does individualism necessitate Libertarian Individualism? Does placing the emphasis on the individual

---

[15] 15 Lewis Sperry Chafer, *Systematic Theology* (1948; repr., Grand Rapids: Kregel Publications, 1993), 1:119.

over the corporate necessitate that each individual feel liberty to act independently of the corporate structure? Thankfully, there is no necessary link between the two sociologically, philosophically, or biblically.

Sociological Perspective: Horizontal and Vertical Individualism

Recent research on scales of individualism provides some illumination on this point. Triandis, followed by a new wave of social scientists, has proposed that two types of Individualism ought to be distinguished.[16]

> First, horizontal individualism (HI) reflects an independent/same self-construal (people view themselves as equal but independent of one another). Second, vertical individualism (VI) is purported to reflect an independent/different self-construal (people view themselves as unequal but independent). Similarly, horizontal collectivism (HC) reflects an interdependent/same self-construal whereas vertical collectivism (VC) reflects an interdependent/different self-construal.[17]

Triandis' model proposes that collectivists envision themselves as "aspects of an in-group," whereas individualists conceive of themselves as autonomous.[18] However, within individualism there are those cultures which envision the autonomous individual as essentially equal with others (HI) and those which envision each individual as inherently different and unequal (VI).[19]

---

[16] T. M. Singelis et al., "Horizontal and Vertical Dimensions of Individualism and Collectivism: A Theoretical and Measurement Refinement," *Cross-Cultural Research* 29 (1995): 240–275.

[17] Fuan Li and Lerzan Aksoy, "Dimensionality of Individualism–Collectivism and Measurement Equivalence of Triandis and Gelfand's Scale," *Journal of Business and Psychology* 21 (2007): 316.

[18] Singelis, "Horizontal and Vertical Dimensions of Individualism and Collectivism: A Theoretical and Measurement Refinement," 244-45.

[19] Ibid., 245. Triandis identifies Australia and Sweden with HI and France and the United States with VI. Ibid., 246.

Although some problems have been found with the scale,[20] such that it should not be taken as an infallible guide, the basic distinctions to date have been validated. What it contributes to this discussion is the possibility that the individual can be considered as an independent entity and still have a variety of relationships with the collective. Conceiving of themselves first as autonomous and then as part of a larger in-group does not necessitate the complete subordination of the group to the individual in all flavors of individualism. It is possible to both have a robust emphasis on the individual and an understanding of the individuals place as one among equals.

Philosophical Perspective: Johann Fichte and Intersubjectivity

Sociologically, there is no reason why individualism must necessitate a Libertarian expression of individualism. In other words, it is possible to place the emphasis on the individual without mandating that each individual disregard the larger collective to which they belong. What Triandis observes empirically has been proposed philosophically as well. Surveying the development of a Western philosophy of autonomy, Macken comments on the philosophy of Johann Gottlieb Fichte, a rough contemporary of Kant and a founder of German Idealism:

> It would be a mistake to see in Fitchte's principle of absolute self-determination a radical individualism. The contrary is in fact the case. Absolute self-determination is an ideal which is man's ethical task to strive after but which he cannot attain. His progress is striving after it is, however, the common task of the human community. Fichte held that the Ego could only posit itself as an individual. But the notion of the individual and of his free activity implied a limitation and this limitation implied the notion of other activity on the part of other agents. The very possibility of my becoming aware of my freedom in the first place depends on an impulse from without that summons me to activity. . . . It implies the existence of at least one other rational being that

[20] Li, "Dimensionality of Individualism–Collectivism and Measurement Equivalence of Triandis and Gelfand's Scale."

> summons me to activity but yet leaves me entirely free for self-determination.[21]

In Fitche's view, the individual is the most natural and helpful way to understand the makeup of the corporate. However, this does not necessitate that each individual operates completely independently.

> The conflict implied in radical individualism is resolved by Fichte in a devaluation of the empirical individual in favour of a higher unity. . . .Fichte did not hold to a radical individualism. He developed instead a philosophy of intersubjectivity. My awareness of freedom comes from the encounter with rational beings outside of myself. Ethical progress implies a free community of rational discourse in which empirical individuals yield to the demands of a higher unity.[22]

Biblical Perspective: Intersubjectivity in Psalm 73

Fitche's concept of intersubjectivity mirrors Scripture's own view of the relationship between the individual and the whole. A clear illustration of this is seen in Psalm 73. In this Psalm, Asaph describes his near slip into unbelief caused by the seeming prosperity of those who disregard the Law of God. The Psalm begins in individualistic terms, describing how the author's feet nearly stumbled. Asaph is clearly describing here his personal experience, which continues through the first sixteen verses. Asaph's own observation, though, produces a distorted impression of reality, as seen in the dissonance between verse one, which states as a header that *Elohim* is good to the upright, and verse twelve, which records the summary of his observations that the wicked lack in trouble. However, a stark transition takes place in verses 16-17, where Asaph is moved from being weary of walking in righteousness (16) to understanding the true fate of the unrighteous (17). This transition, though, does not take place because of his own individual musings, but rather happens after he enters the sanctuary of God, almost assuredly the temple. The Psalm does not specify what in the Sanctuary initiated this transition, but it is important that it was a public

---

[21] Macken, *The Autonomy Theme in the Church Dogmatics*, 15.

[22] Ibid., 16,18.

place of corporate worship which righted the Psalmist's distorted vision of the world.

This pattern exactly sums up the Protestant doctrine of the priesthood of all believers. This foundational doctrine of Protestant theology proposes much more than that each believer has direct access to the Father on the basis of union with Christ, but also that each believer serves as a priest to each other.[23] Here we see Fichte's concept of intersubjectivity. Any individual seeking complete independence lacks that stimulus for proper understanding which can only be found when the "empirical individuals yields to the demands of a higher unity."[24]

Individualism and Theonomy

Kant suggested the distinction between autonomy, or ethical action arising from one's will, and heteronomy, submitting to the will of another. Individualistic cultures are naturally suspicious of the later,[25] feeling that this sort of action must be personally disingenuous. However, the Christian understands that one is not simply subject to moral self-governance, but rather as a created being they are subject to the law of God (Ps 119:1-4), a theonomy. Karl Barth, speaking on the subject, states that

> It is not, then, our business to speak of autonomy in dogmatics until we have first made it clear that the theonomy of dogmatics has as its primary counterpart a heteronomy. The 'other law' to which Christian proclamation and therefore first and foremost dogmatics itself is subject, can only be the law of God.

---

[23] Mark Rogers, "A Dangerous Idea? Martin Luther, E.Y. Mullins, and the Priesthood of All Believers," *Westminster Theological Journal* 72 (2010): 122.

[24] Macken, *The Autonomy Theme in the Church Dogmatics*, 18.

[25] "Individuals in collectivists cultures are motivated by other's choices, whereas individuals in individualistic cultures are motivated when they have personal choice." Harry C. Triandis and Michele J. Gelfand, "A Theory of Individualism and Collectivism," in *Handbook of Theories of Social Psychology* (London: Sage Publications, 2012), 508.

> Therefore, the heteronomy to which
> we refer necessarily implies the theonomy.[26]

Because humans are contingent beings, their autonomy is subject to an implied heteronomy, namely "The theonomy of God which wills and decrees as such the autonomy of man."[27]

Contra Libertarian Individualism, each individual is not free to make their own ethical choices, though they are capable of doing so, precisely because this would be a denial of the source of their contingent autonomy, the will of God. Thus human beings, despite being free to be wholly autonomous, are to submit themselves.

If this is true for each individual to his creator, could it not also be true of individuals to others? The Mosaic Law models this parallel, for it establishes the obligation each individual in the covenant has to one another in addition to their obligation to God:

> The fundamental social commandment of the Mosaic corpus, the commandment of Leviticus 19:18, 'Thou shalt love thy neighbor as thyself,' is paradigmatic both of the Mosaic method of legislation and of its goals *vis-à-vis* the integration of the individual in the community. In terms of goals, this commandment both rests upon and fosters individuality: for it is addressed to the individual moral agent and seeks the good of other individuals. Yet in so doing, it establishes bonds of fellowship and fellow feeling . . . an identification of the good of another as one's own concern.[28]

This principle is patterned for us in the prototypical human, Christ Himself, "who, though he was in the form of God, did not regard equality with God

---

[26] Karl Barth, *Church Dogmatics*, ed. G. W. Bromiley and Thomas Torrance, trans. G. W. Bromiley, vol. 2.2 (London ; T & T Clark International, 2004), 815.

[27] Ibid., 1.2:180.

[28] Lenn E. Goodman, "The Individual and the Community in the Normative Traditions of Judaism," in *Autonomy and Judaism*, ed. Daniel Frank (Albany: State University of New York Press, 1992), 80.

as something to be exploited, but emptied himself, taking the form of a slave, being born in human likeness" (Phil 2:6-7).

> The perfection of God's giving Himself to man in the person of Jesus Christ consists in the fact that far from merely playing with man, far from merely moving or using him, far from merely dealing with him as an object, this self-giving sets man up as a subject, awakens him to genuine individuality and autonomy, frees him, makes him a king, so that in his rule the kingly rule of God Himself attains form and revelation. How can there be any possible rivalry here, let along usurpation? How can there be any question of a conflict between theonomy and autonomy?[29]

Here then is the pattern for proper human interaction between the individual and the whole. If any human were autonomous, it would be Christ. However, His autonomy did not mandate that He act merely in accord with His own will or for His own desires. Rather, in submitting to the Father, He worked our good for our salvation. Humans then are surely autonomous, in that we are individual units, and to some extent are capable of freely choosing to act in accordance with our own will. We are free, however, it is a "freedom consisting in the fact that in its autonomy it recognizes and acknowledges that it is wholly and utterly responsible to God."[30] This responsibility to God entails a similar attitude towards those to whom God as Creator has knit us to—not the Church only but also humanity in general. A well-developed attitude of intersubjectivity provides the key by which a proper emphasis may be placed on the individual without over-inflating either its autonomy from others nor its responsibility to impulses outside of itself. In short, intersubjectivity allows individualism to pass a biblical evaluation.

---

[29] Ibid., 1.2:179.

[30] Ibid., 1.2:121.

CHAPTER 5

IMPLICATIONS AND CONCLUSIONS

Implications

A study of individualism and the Bible provides an excellent example of how culture both shapes our understanding of Scripture and ought to be shaped by it. Every reading of Scripture is an encultured reading, and good students of the Bible must be aware of where their cultural bias might lead them astray. For instance, a reader in an individualistic culture might inadvertently downplay important corporate aspects of Scripture. However, this study has shown that different cultures can bring fresh emphases to the biblical text, and debunks the theory that any reading from a culture different from the Bible is necessarily suspect. Theologians are right at times to criticize aspects of individualism; however, they ought to be more precise about what aspect of individualism is dissonant with Christianity, rather than condemning the whole system. Too often critics have proposed that because individualistic cultures are culturally removed from the world of the Bible, that by necessity makes readings with an individualistic emphasis suspect. This paper has attempted to show that these criticisms are unfounded.

A reading of Scripture influenced by individualism does indeed highlight several important aspects of theology. It features the significance of each human in the divine program because if the *imago dei*. This significance is clearly seen in personal responsibility for both sin and righteousness, faith and unbelief. The Bible elevates the significant of the individual, and so should we as well.

Another important implication for the study of individualism is in the realm of ecclesiology, and indeed it is this arena that criticisms of it are most often levied. The church is undeniably a corporate entity, such that its worship is normally referred to as corporate worship. In this regard, an individualistic worldview will significantly affect how one envisions the individuals which make up a church interacting with the corporate.

Individualism implies that the individual is the level on which change takes place. Miller makes this point emphatically, stating that "The individual—not the community, not public opinion, not external environmental forces—is the source of new ideas that enable society to make changes for the achievement of ideals."[1] The importance of this observation for church workers cannot be understated. Despite the New Testament addressing churches as a whole, one must understand that change comes from the individuals in the church. Change must start by developing individuals, not at the church-wide level. Too often, leaders are tempted to enact change in their organizations at the organizational level by somehow altering the organizational culture. Individualism implies that change only comes from and through the individual members of the corporate body.

Furthermore, this observation is consistent with Scriptures own teaching on spiritual formation. Paul states that he struggles for his "children" until "Christ is formed in you" (Gal 4:19). Granted, the pronoun is plural, but it is consistent with our understanding of the union and communion of each believer with Christ to understand this to mean Christ is formed in each

---

[1] "Individualism as we understand it always involves novelty, the creativity of an enterprising person who is instrumental in effecting new and, purportedly, more effective ways of achieving socially acceptable goals by using means in accord with our traditional values. The individual is an innovator whose new proposal is directed to his community, small or large." David L. Miller, *Individualism: Personal Achievement and the Open Society* (Austin: University of Texas Press, 1967), 3.

individual believer. It is the goal of Christian instruction that each believer become fully mature as Christ is formed in them. (Col 1:27-28, 4:12). Since

> Individualism is a theory which maintains that selves or persons are the loci of human-value dignity and worth, and that as individuals they constitute the source of new ideas whose practical application is necessary for the growth of society and for the emergence of new values shared by the participants in the group of which the individuals having the new ideas are members.[2]

Individualism then places the proper focus of this transformative process. The church as a corporate body only grows and transforms as Christ is formed within each believer. The implication of individualism for Christian leaders is significant in this regard. The emphasis must not be primarily on corporate structure as the means of spiritual growth, but rather on the spiritual formation of each individual.

However, although individualism does place a proper emphasis on the value and role of the individual in the corporate, this emphasis can also be inflated. Many in Western cultures have adopted a form of individualism which idolizes the individual choice at the expense of the corporate wellbeing, and against this attitude Christian thinkers have properly leveled criticism. Some for instance have correlated individual autonomy, an aspect of individualism, with "a decrease in parish involvement."[3] It is the nature of sin to overinflate the self, and thus one symptom of individualism which must be recognized is the tendency to promote that a Christian can live a full-fledged Christian life apart from, or in contrary to, a corporate body. It

---

[2] Ibid., 75.

[3] "Personal autonomy thus has not only led to a decline in parish involvement—by increased individual over collective-expressiveness and increased secondary over primary identity—but it has also led to an alteration in the meaning of that involvement." Phillip E. Hammond, *Religion and Personal Autonomy* (Columbia: University of South Carolina Press, 1992), 8.

is not antithetical to individualism for the individual Christian to believe in the importance of incorporation into the church local and universal. Thus, this facet of Libertarian Individualism must be resisted.

Conclusion

In conclusion, does the Bible support the basic tenants of Individualism? The Scriptures certainly do support the notion that the individual human exists and that it has value in God's sight. One must also conclude that each individual has been imbued with a certain degree of autonomy. On the other hand, the Bible also contains many features common to collectivism, such as the clear binding of each person of faith to the people of God in a common hope and destiny, as well as the command to make choices which prefer the group over the will of the individual (Phil 2:4).

It should be noted that individualism can largely be defended on the basis of several important classic Protestant doctrines. Protestantism has distinctly emphasized the standing of the individual before God, both as individually guilty of sin and the salvation personally available to each. This is not to discount the emphasis in both Testaments on the salvation of the corporate. However, the fact that each individual appropriates salvation based upon an individual act of faith is indelible to Protestant doctrine. Additionally, the doctrines of the priesthood of all believers and *sola scriptura,* both critical to Reformation thinking, have significant implications for individualism. For this reason, it is not surprising that individualism has incubated in Protestant cultures. It should also leave one wary that they can wholesale reject individualism without harm to Protestant dogma.

In the name of not defaulting to the coveted middle, synthetic position, one ought to conclude that a thorough biblical evaluation supports the basic tenets of individualism, although with some caveats and warnings, as one might expect from any cultural system. The Bible upholds the unique value of each human individual, and for this reason, an emphasis on the individual instead of the corporate is legitimate. However, any flavor of individualism which requires or celebrates that an individual disregard corporate entities must be rejected. Only an individualism with a healthy understanding of intersubjectivity can truly be supported biblically. However, since it is doubtful both socially and philosophically that this is a necessary aspect of individualism, it should be considered as a warning, but need not lead to the rejection of the system as a whole.

As finite creatures, any human worldview will struggle to hold together the totality of God's created order. Even when biblically influenced, human modes of thinking will always emphasize some truths at the expense of others. Individualism is, of course, no different. However, individualism does pass enough of a Biblical evaluation that it can be uphold as a legitimate cultural framework.

BIBLIOGRAPHY

Ameriks, Karl, and Dieter Sturma, eds. *The Modern Subject: Conceptions of the Self in Classical German Philosophy*. Albany: State University of New York Press, 1995.

Athanasius. *The Letters of Saint Athanasius Concerning the Holy Spirit*. Translated by C.R.B. Shapland. London: Epworth Press, 1951.

Augustine of Hippo. "On the Trinity." In *St. Augustin: On the Holy Trinity, Doctrinal Treatises, Moral Treatises*, edited by Philip Schaff, translated by Arthur West Haddan. A Select Library of the Nicene and Post-Nicene Fathers of the Christian Church 3. Buffalo: Christian Literature Company, 1887.

Audi, Robert, ed. *The Cambridge Dictionary of Philosophy*. 3rd ed. Cambridge: Cambridge University Press, 1999.

Barth, Karl. *Church Dogmatics*. Edited by G. W. Bromiley and Thomas Torrance. Translated by G. W. Bromiley. Vol. 2.2. London; T & T Clark International, 2004.

Bauer, Walter. *A Greek-English Lexicon of the New Testament and Other Early Christian Literature.* Revised and edited by Frederick W. Danker. 3rd ed. Chicago: University of Chicago Press, 2000.

Bellah, Robert. *Habits of the Heart: Individualism and Commitment in American Life*. Berkeley: University of California Press, 1985.

Blackburn, Simon, ed. *The Oxford Dictionary of Philosophy*. Oxford: Oxford University Press, 1994.

Block, James. "Looking Forward: Hobbes on Modernity." *New Political Science* 22 (2000): 411–415.

Burnett, Gary W. *Paul and the Salvation of the Individual.* Leiden: Brill, 2001.

Chafer, Lewis Sperry. *Systematic Theology*. 1948. Reprint, Grand Rapids: Kregel Publications, 1993.

Chillingsworth, William. *The Religion of the Protestants: A Safe Way to Salvation*. Oxford: Leonard Lichfield, 1638.

Cohen, Anthony P. *Alternative Anthropology of Identity*. New York: Routledge, 1994.

Dodd, Brian. "Romans 1:17—A Crux Interpretum for the ΠΙΣΤΙΣ ΧΡΙΣΤΟΥ Debate." *Journal of Biblical Literature* 113 (1994): 470–73.

Dunson, Ben C. "The Individual and Community in Twentieth- and Twenty-First-Century Pauline Scholarship." *Currents in Biblical Research* 9 (2010): 63–97.

Fichte, Johann Gottlieb. *Foundations of Natural Right*. Edited by Frederick Neuhouser. Translated by Michael Baur. Cambridge: Cambridge University Press, 2000.

Frank, Daniel H., ed. *Autonomy and Judaism: The Individual and the Community in Jewish Philosophical Thought*. Albany: State University of New York Press, 1992.

Gelpi, Donald L., ed. *Beyond Individualism: Toward a Retrieval of Moral Discourse in America*. Notre Dame: University of Notre Dame Press, 1989.

George, Timothy. *The Theology of the Reformers*. Nashville: Broadman & Holman, 1988.

Gregory, Brad S. *The Unintended Reformation: How a Religious Revolution Secularized Society*. Cambridge: Belknap Press, 2012.

Hammond, Phillip E. *Religion and Personal Autonomy*. Columbia: University of South Carolina Press, 1992.

Hieert, Dennis, and Edmund Neuffeld. "Me and Jesus? Countering Individualism with a More Collectivist Reading of Scripture." Paper Presented at the 46th Annual Meeting of the Evangelical Theological Society, Chicago, IL, November 17-19, 1994.

Hofstede, Geert. *Culture's Consequences: International Differences in Work-Related Values*. Abr. Ed. Newbury Park: Sage, 1984.

Hunt, Lynn, trans. and ed. *The French Revolution and Human Rights: A Brief Documentary History*. New York: St. Martin's, 1996.

Johnson, Aubrey. *The Vitality of the Individual in the Thought of Ancient Israel*. Cardiff: University of Wales Press, 1964.

Kagıtçıbası, Cigdem. "Individualism and Collectivism." In *Handbook of Cross-Cultural Psychology: Social Behaviors and Applications*, 1-50. Edited by John Berry, et al. 2nd ed. Boston: Allyn and Bacon, 1997.

Kaminsky, Joel S. *Corporate Responsibility in the Hebrew Bible.* Journal for the Study of the Old Testament Supplemental Series, vol. 196. Sheffield: Sheffield Academic Press, 1995.

Kavanaugh, John. "Autonomous Individualism." *America* 196 (2007): 8.

Koehler, Ludwig, Walter Baumgartner, M. E. J. Richardson, and Johann Jakob Stamm. *The Hebrew and Aramaic Lexicon of the Old Testament.* Leiden: E.J. Brill, 2000.

Li, Fuan, and Lerzan Aksoy. "Dimensionality of Individualism–Collectivism and Measurement Equivalence of Triandis and Gelfand's Scale." *Journal of Business and Psychology* 21 (2007): 313–329.

Luther, Martin. *Luther's Works*, vol. 34. Edited by Helmut Lehmann. Translated by Lewis W. Spitz. American ed. Philadelphia: Muhlenberg Press, 1960.

Macken, Eric. "In Defense of Individualism." *Ethical Theory and Moral Practice* 2 (1999): 87–115.

Malina, Bruce J. *The New Testament World: Insights from Cultural Anthropology.* 3rd ed. Louisville: Westminster John Knox Press, 2001.

Merrill, Eugene. *Deuteronomy.* The New American Commentary, vol. 4. Nashville: Broadman & Holman Publishers, 1994.

Miller, David L. *Individualism: Personal Achievement and the Open Society.* Austin: University of Texas Press, 1967.

Morris, Colin. *The Discovery of the Individual 1050-1200.* 2nd ed. Toronto: University of Toronto Press, 1987.

Musschenga, Albert W. and Anton van Harskamp, eds. *The Many Faces of Individualism.* Leuven: Peeters, 2001.

Osterley, W. O. E., and Theodore H. Robinson. *An Introduction to the Books of the Old Testament.* London: Society for Promoting Christian Knowledge, 1961.

Pelikan, Jaroslav, et al. *Individualism and Social Responsibility*. Dallas: The University of Texas at Dallas Press, 1994.

Robertson, Archibald, and Alfred Plummer. *A Critical and Exegetical Commentary on the First Epistle of St Paul to the Corinthians*. International Critical Commentary. Edinburgh: T&T Clark, 1914.

Rogers, Mark. "A Dangerous Idea? Martin Luther, E.Y. Mullins, and the Priesthood of All Believers." *Westminster Theological Journal* 72 (2010): 119–34.

Sampson, E. E. "Reinterpreting Individualism and Collectivism. Their Religious Roots and Monologic versus Dialogic Person-Other Relationship." *The American Psychologist 55* (2000).

Schimmack, Ulrich. "Individualism: A Valid and Important Dimension of Cultural Differences Between Nations." *Personality and Social Psychology Review* 9 (2005): 17–31.

Schneewind, Jerome B. *The Invention of Autonomy: A History of Modern Moral Philosophy*. Cambridge: Cambridge University Press, 1997.

Singelis, Theodore M., Harry C. Triandis, Dharm P.S. Bhawuk, and Michele J. Gelfand. "Horizontal and Vertical Dimensions of Individualism and Collectivism: A Theoretical and Measurement Refinement." *Cross-Cultural Research* 29 (1995): 240–275.

Thiselton, Anthony C. *The First Epistle to the Corinthians: A Commentary on the Greek Text*. New International Greek Testament Commentary. Grand Rapids: Eerdmans, 2000.

de Tocqueville, Alexis. *Democracy in America*. Translated by Henry Reeve. New York: J & H G. Langley, 1840.

Triandis, Harry C. "Individualism-Collectivism and Personality." *Journal of Personality* 69 (2001): 907–924.

Triandis, Harry C., and Michele J. Gelfand. "A Theory of Individualism and Collectivism." In *Handbook of Theories of Social Psychology*, 498–520. London: Sage Publications, 2012.

Wolff, Hans Walter. *Anthropology of the Old Testament*. Translated by Margaret Kohl. Philadelphia: Fortress Press, 1974.

World Value Survey. "Wave 6 (2010-2014)." Accessed November 15, 2015. http://www.worldvaluessurvey.org/WVSDocumentationWV6.jsp/.

Zerubavel, E., and E. R. Smith. "Transcending Cognitive Individualism." *Social Psychology Quarterly* 73 (2010): 321–25.

www.ingramcontent.com/pod-product-compliance
Ingram Content Group UK Ltd.
Pitfield, Milton Keynes, MK11 3LW, UK
UKHW041916190726
13854UKWH00003B/1268